L'appel du Vide

THE CALL OF THE VOID

Sarah AA

Library of Congress Control Number: 2019918071
ISBN: Softcover 978-1-5437-5519-0
eBook 978-1-5437-5532-9

Print information available on the last page.

To order additional copies of this book, contact
Toll Free 800 101 2657 (Singapore)
Toll Free 1 800 81 7340 (Malaysia)
orders.singapore@partridgepublishing.com

www.partridgepublishing.com/singapore

CONTENTS

JUST FOR YOU

Be Silent

Start observing.

When they call you names,

When they portray their insecurities on you,

Be silent.

Start listening.

Tell yourself you don't need to be fixed.

Even if you can't convince yourself at the time,

Tell yourself you're allowed to make mistakes.

And when you become your worst enemy,

Right then, learn to become your biggest fan.

Memories

The past doesn't hurt us.

It's our interpretation of the past that does.

What the past leaves behind,

Leftovers.

Happy Blue Pills

Am I addicted to them? Or addicted to the idea of their existence?

Learn to exercise pain in order to appreciate pleasure.

Just because no one knows,

Just because the memories faded to you

Does not make it right.

I guess I would rather just push it

And let it immerse in other memories,

Not knowing that my body still remembers.

It remembers.

Complaining about the Ashes

As they said, I am toxic,

And you still chose to touch me.

Don't blame me if you try to light a cigarette and then catch fire.

My soul is a little dark slave

That I caged in my little dark basement.

I still carry a whip and a gun when I choose to feed it.

I know that my soul is so much bigger than the frame my body drew for it.

Every time I wake up, I have to look at my hands to make sure they are still there.

From Me to Me

You seem to love me more when the lights are off.

Let's indulge in the love we created; I don't want to be allowed to say, "If only."

I'd rather fall in remorse so deeply to the point where I hate myself.

I'd rather regret so hard till it takes over me, so I know it's my mistake.

I can't say you're at fault, but I hope you understand that my anger must spew in all directions in order for me to grieve.

I hope you understand.

I hope you still love me.

My mind hates the love my heart carries.

Let's love till the simplest of things become the most complicated.

Let's love till we are restless.

Let's love till "ordinary" gets bored of us.

Let's love till we explode.

It's so liberating when someone starts to fade,

When your heart finally decides to let go,

Remembering you can be yourself without them.

Once a baby bird learns how to fly, it gets a taste of freedom. And it rarely comes back to thank the teacher, the mother. And that is why by nature, most of the time, she forgets. And so should you.

You're allowed to miss them; they're just not allowed to know.

So grieve as if they were dead.

I learned to love others before loving myself.

I still don’t know what that means.

Love makes us believe in things we never did.

Love makes us hate.

I was 5 years old, playing hide-and-seek. They used to cover my eyes with a thick veil and ask me not to cheat. Put me against the wall while my enemies plotted against me and started to spread out. When I would start searching for them, I'd forget that I was wearing a veil and start relying on my senses, as if not being able to see was my natural state. So I simply listened, felt, and I started remembering every crease in my house. Sometimes I would tilt my head back and begin to cheat, listening for the very soft murmur of giggles of my 5-year-old cousins while they told each other to be quiet.

This is what happens to people who are in love. They forget that they are blind and rely simply on the senses of their hearts. Try to remind them that they can listen even if they cannot see. Giggle around them, so you can help them cheat. Remind them that they are unhappy; they are in love. Hold their hands and guide them through the creases of the unfamiliar home; make them feel the cracks through their fingers. They will remember the feeling of broken windows out of anger and frustration. They will see that their mothers have suffered, and so they have suffered too. Their grandmothers have suffered, and so their mothers have suffered too. Try staying as silent as possible, and hush all the others around you. Simply show them; allow them to listen and feel. Allow them to break the chain. Remind them that they are capable of being happy with someone else.

They don’t deserve to be in a dismantling house even if they cannot see it. And when they finally decide to take off the veil, allow them to cry. Because the house meant something to them, they thought it was different. They were deceived.

Becoming the Story

Love is an immense feeling of hunger to fit exactly into someone's puzzle, forgetting that your body naturally fits perfectly into many other people's puzzles.

It's not choosing to say that you fit perfectly with them.

It's not realizing that you fit with others too,

letting the rest of humanity be marginalized, while you and they slowly start to become the main words on the page.

Had people telling me my love is too pure,

Saying it like it's a bad thing.

Like I carry poison in my veins, waiting to be triggered,

Waiting for something to pulse it through me.

They say it like it's a bad thing.

As if pain was an obligation that simply is a part of pleasure

And not a completely different word.

They say some hearts love too much

But forget to use it metaphorically.

Because how can you ever love too much?

Let the love consume you.

Destroy yourself before others.

I think you should forgive yourself.

Love forgot how meaningful it is until it met us.

You forgot how meaningful love is until you met me.

I forgot how meaningful you are until you met her.

You’re allowed to feel grateful and still feel unhappy.

I still expect people to erase the handcuffs I drew for myself.

To set me free.

Help, my voice is too loud for me.

I'm suffocating on my own vocals.

aBOUT US

Sometimes I wish you hugged me closer that day, and other times, I wish our eyes never met.

After all, I was never as important as your own feelings. You made that perfectly clear, but you can't think and love at the same time.

There were moments when my world was collapsing, and the thought of you kept me sane.

There are moments when I think of you, and my world starts collapsing.

I would be the liar if I said kissing you was like kissing anyone.

This is the first time I kissed someone, and I didn't hear silence.

I heard fireworks, like the universe was applauding us.

You made me fear the moon.

You're the loneliest I have ever been

Because when you hold me,

All I recognize is every second that I have not been held.

I still look for you in places we have been. Picture our silhouettes merging into one beautiful shadow. I see us in other people, and I just wonder if you still see it too.

I folded myself beneath him, and he carried me as if I were his ego. He lathered me with the convenience of my existence. Made me recognize the persistence of my love. Chained me to my own presence, and my Lego thoughts rattled in my basket of a brain because when you love, your brain is simply a rattling basket.

The bittersweet aftertaste of your tongue draining my essence into yours makes me want to kiss all seventeen billion people on this planet to get that feeling to go away.

We decided to settle for an empty room and let it be a part of us.

We had nothing to make of it, so we sat on the floor.

And our words slowly started to fill the hollow corners of our tight little room until we were suffocating on our own laughter.

But then the echoes became louder than our own voices.

And so the walls began to crumble around us.

And we lay there in an emotionless, dark void, floating on the rest of the world's despair.

He made my sunflowers bloom exactly the way they should,

Pointing to the direction of the sun.

But then he knew they were hiding something; they weren't looking at him.

“I did it for the both of us,” you tried to tell me.

Because that is much easier than saying you indulged in your own selfish needs.

I'm not sure what is more painful.

He hits the wall once, twice, and maybe even three times,

As if the walls will not absorb his energy.

He thinks he is stronger than the cement built by men who were only sweating peace.

Simple men.

His anger spews from his knuckles directly into the chambers of paint, and the vibrations gravitate so angrily, and for a second, they scream.

And they come back so calm.

Serene.

They come back with only peace.

I'm not sure what is more painful—

knowing that it will always end like this or that I picked up your bad habit.

I know that you are curious. You want to know the maximum someone can give you. You lost so much from yourself and look for it in others. Because maybe they have something you need.

It's ok if you hurt me, precious.

It's ok if you want to grow alone.

And it's ok if I wasn't part of your plan.

We both knew.

We knew so well it hurt.

But it's ok.

I may not be the person you chose.

But at least I kept my promises,

Which is ironic, given that you constantly praised your own words,

Telling me that you kept them,

Preserved them in a glass box.

I thought I was your museum, right, precious?

We both wanted too much from ourselves.

I guess our love was too big.

Our love was explosive; it killed.

But at least I know I will keep my promises.

What about you, precious?

I guess you forgot your persistent hands crawling on my body, and I let you because I was explosive.

But I didn't think my vulnerability would get the best of me.

I guess what I mean to say is I didn't think you'd walk away this easily.

This fast.

Did you even try?

Have a penny because I'm desperate to know what was going on in your mind.

But isn't that the best part, craving something you don't have, can't have?

But I guess you gave up, or dare I say, you're tired?

It wasn't enough, right, Daddy?

But at least I kept my promises.

What about you, precious?

I lay out all the sharp objects in front of me. I stare at them intently. I think how much I want new scars. You stole my scars, didn't you? I used to feel as though they were my survival. Now, every time I look at them, all I see is your fingers gently tracing them, making them yours. I ask you to stop, stop taking my survival away from me. You don't seem to understand because I see you trace them with your gaze. You stole my scars; now all I can think of is making new ones. I just wanted them to be mine.

You made me forget my own body.

You made me forget how to love myself.

I had to teach myself, but I can't help but remember your hips forcefully spreading me.

Pinning me in place, your face, it said I love you.

But your body said this is your place.

I was scared to look at myself in the mirror,

Scared of my organs decomposing and landing on the floor.

I guess in that moment I was your territory and nothing more.

I'm jealous that when you look away, your eyes don't belong to me anymore.

Omission is a form of lying.

He just chooses his words wisely.

But I studied him,

And I choose to respond with my actions;

And he chooses to lie with his actions.

Just remember that omission is a form of lying.

Just because I didn't say anything does not mean I was silent.

In that Moment

Where the moon and the sun collided and I was leaving,

I mouthed, “I love you,” through the foggy glass window.

I knew that things would never be the same right in that moment.

The headlights were like an ocean, ready to be the high tide of my loneliness.

Thank you for wishing me all the best.

Thank you for pretending to have the right intentions.

At least you cared enough to pretend, while many simply admired the idea of me.

“You’re stronger than you think.”

This is a poem about your deception.

You are what deceit is made of.

You may not think so, but I replay in my head the number of times you said, “I will be there.

When you’re down, I will be there,”

You said more times than I can count.

At least with the others, they never made any promises.

I know you well enough to know that you chose to walk away because you couldn't handle leaving so many times.

I'm sorry; I wanted to handle the pain for you, but how can I when you didn't.

I'm sorry I lied.

But this poem is about your deception.

I hope you know that my heart still looks for you when I'm down.

Thank you for deceiving my heart and then wishing me all the best.

Forget the promises; they will never be real.

Let them burn with the remainders of him.

You are the reason he breathes.

He looked for parts of his mother inside you.

Now let him look for parts of you inside the rest of them.

You manufactured every sentence to be so beautifully painful.

I guess you did learn from the best; finally, I am a proud teacher.

You got to touch the line between pleasure and pain.

How exhilarating.

You allowed me to love you because it was convenient.

Because you were lonely; but I was ok.

And now I'm lonely.

I filled you with love till love was scared of its own meaning.

And now I'm lonely,

And you're ok.

How convenient.

You think it's simple to forgive.

You assume that forgiveness comes with amnesia.

You think the trust I once gave you is still in your possession.

You said, "I'm sorry," but where is it?

What can I do with your mere application of words that your tongue is so used to saying, but in your heart, you simply desire what you once had?

You just miss, but you are not sorry.

You did not feel.

You have no idea.

I forgive you but never like before.

Stammering in objects that carry your essence. It's amazing how they are still here but you aren't. They kept promises you didn't.

They feel but you don't.

I hope my touch made everyone feel less of who they are to you.

And so we dwelled on our blood-stained sheets and rubbed our scents all over the furniture to be remembered.

I hope she poisons you with her ivy touch. I hope her fingers mimic mine when she glides them down your back. And then she digs her witchy nails through the sheets of your skin.

I hope she poisons you.

Your feeling is something I wish I could touch.

ABOUT THEM

The day he asked me to come over,

"Please," you say.

But I'm not sure if you're asking for permission or consent.

The smile you see on my face, it means I'm scared.

When I look up, it does not mean go ahead.

To everyone who is afraid of the walls around them,

They will press against your face, suffocating your body.

Fight back until they are afraid of you.

Put the razor down.

Your body will always repair, but the scars won't.

Notice the way he raises his voice to be louder than hers.

Notice the way he lowers his voice so it's stronger than her silence.

Notice the smudged ink all over the pages of her books.

Notice her prayers infiltrated with tears.

Notice the everlasting scars buried in her story coated with fear of being bigger

Herself.

Please forgive me if my pain speaks before me.

My scars are still acquainted with the moon.

As soon as all the stars align,

They become wolves.

When I was a child,

I would imagine them training me to be a princess.

They would put the book on my head and ask me to walk,

Balancing between my body and the book

But never reading the book.

Never taught me how to talk.

I'm afraid of the day I stare at the title of that book and not understand what it means

Even though it was right over my brain.

They'd teach me to keep my chin up, shoulders back.

Never teach me how to keep it high

Or how to look left or right.

I imagine my neck like a rusting pole;

If I move, it makes an agitating sound that only I can hear.

The book is on my head, but is it really?

My brain can't get a grasp of it.

The day I realized I grew up

Is the day I went to my mother and looked her in her precious eyes and said,

“Mommy, I don’t think I want to be a princess anymore.”

I've heard so much about me, and somewhere along those words, I forgot who I was, and now I want to learn how to love me again. But my heart already occupies too many; it cannot carry its own.

Artists are complicated beings; be gentle. They have themselves to deal with.

Everyone is an artist.

Don't blame time for all the moments you choose not to live.

A halo emerged from each of them.

They all reflected and absorbed colors that could not be seen,

Tracing them so delicately.

And then I watched them

Steal each other's halo colors,

Sharing the spotlight of existence.

The greatest power we don't realize we have is words.

One day my mother came to me and told me my father had been shot.

I bowed my head, and the tears started to grow in my eyes.

I looked at her and asked,

"He's dead, but did he die with bravery or with fear?"

She went silent.

He's dead, but did he die with bravery or with fear?

Did he die chest up and head up, like the soldier that he was?

Did he die proud and belligerent, knowing he was dying for the cause of other people?

Or did he die running, running with anxiety and scared of the feeling that his soul might float with no purpose?

Did he put his gun down?

Or was he persistent that his death must be avenged with his own pistol?

Did he put his gun down?

Your father has been shot.

But did he die proudly and in agony.

We've all been shot.

Ask your friends whether they died proudly or with agony.

Ask them if they put their guns down.

If they gave up that simply.

Everyone around you is dead.

Everyone around you has been shot.

You just don't know it yet.

To all the people who said I couldn't make it, thank you for pushing me to make it.

To all the people who said I could make it, I'm sorry I didn't make it.

They all said I was too much.

I never understood what too much really meant.

It didn't take long for them to make me realize

that too much really meant not enough.

Too much meant they couldn't handle me;

too much meant give less.

Less confidence, less body, less face, less everything.

Too much meant staple your eyes to the floor, take less space, take the least space possible.

Be invisible.

Be red, not red like fire, red like shy, red like you you're too much.

It means shut the fuck up when you're spoken to; keep it to yourself.

You might as well not exist because you're just too much.

If they thought I was too much back then, they should see me now.

Little do they know that I picked myself up, alone.

Leave the door open to those who want to exit.

Make sure they know that you never cry.

Make sure they know that feminine emotions don't exist.

Make sure they know that you are already complete.

My womanhood.

“Men can like two women at once,” you said to me. My arteries started to melt; my heart slowly started sinking into my guts.

Involuntarily, all I could think of was, *I’m not the only one*.

Even though you held me like I was ...

Not realizing what you were saying is women are designed to be loyal, designed to obey, designed to love in extremes and not quantities.

As if the only way to show if they care about me is by the show of hands.

Mother, I want to be an artist.

I want to spread the sorrow that holds my eyes.

Stacks of paper are stumbling in front of me, yelling that I'm not good enough in bright red ink.

But mother, I want to be an artist.

Her face only reeks of disappointment.

She thinks I am blind to the 'real world.'

Yet, Uber drivers are still telling me about their master's degrees and how their dreams crumbled, crashing into the waves of other people's desires

Mother, I want to be an artist.

Validation.

He wore her on his sleeve, not realizing he looked feminine. He looked exactly like the muscular man that he was, holding himself up with tight metal poles, not realizing that they were rusting. He heard them creak the minute she said no. "But you're mine," he said. "I wore you with full will and power, and now it's time for the world to see how much time it consumed from me to accept wearing you." As if she was begging him, as if there weren't a hundred other gloves staring at him from the store window, asking him to keep them warm. Then she felt obligated to be worn by him because he, he paid for her presence, and it was time for her to do her job. Keep him satisfied with her presence. Refusing would accelerate his anger. Do your job, woman. You said yes once, so what's stopping you now?

Watch them look at you as if you were a mistake.

As if carrying you would break their bones, as if they didn't already enjoy the grip of your jaw while it creaks.

Hold your pride, and put it on.

Let it be the only piece of clothing you own.

Because they did that too.

They tried to tell you that their existence meant protection, as if you didn't inhale and exhale normally when they were not there.

They will try to tell you they fixed you, but be aware that you were never broken.

Make sure you hold your head higher than the time you were ashamed of yourself, and they gently placed their fingers beneath your chin to lift it up.

And if you are unable to do so, raise your hands, and practice on infinite mirrors until your head hold its own grip.

You did that.

You had that much control over a living creature.

Say it with pride.

And when they try to pretend that it doesn't take two to tango,

offer them sympathy because they haven't discovered their places yet.

Allow them to lie, even if lying isn't part of your ethics.

Realize that they are lying for themselves.

Allow them to lie because at one point, you allowed them to love you.

“Don’t spread your filth.”

And so I did exactly as they asked, carried it around till it started decomposing with the air particles and others seemed to inhale it.

In a tornado of unspoken words and broken human parts,

They still stare at women as if they were meant to be devoured by eyes.

A woman who will do the job.

An unopinionated, unthoughtful woman who will not see behind his lies.

She still smells her aura when he walks past her, ungrateful and sighing.

They all feel entitled to take what they want and go.

Empowerment, validation, sex, support—

So take what you want and go.

And when they criticize you for playing their games,

Tell them the many words that they once told you.

"You're acting crazy."

"What are you talking about?"

"You really think I would do that?"

They told me not to lie.

Yet they claim that my mother's bruises came out of clumsiness.

But I've seen the way she walks by him,

Staring at the direction he waves his fists.

They told me not to steal,

But I've seen the way he looks at her,

As if he's done nothing to her quavering body, piercing every part of her skin merely to say that he bought her, she is his.

They told me not to swear,

But I heard his filthy tongue shaking the walls of our wallpaper house, quaking the bases that this house was built on.

When they ask you about happiness, make sure to show them how they taught you to smile.

And so I saw miserable faces on roller-coaster rides.

They all teach you to smile out of compliments,

out of obligations.

And so I saw miserable places with roller-coaster faces.

It irritates me to write about all of you. I'm giving you the immortality you don't deserve.

What a waste of precious art.

How will I live on when you're the only ones being written down?

You look at me, your eyes full of concern.

Though this concern resembles purity,

I can feel them burning my skin.

"Take it out on paper," you say,

"Never on yourself."

So I use every single metaphor that comes to my mind.

So many ways to restate the obvious.

I gave my soul for many to feed on.

All of them bit off more than they could chew.

And I gave them more than I could afford to give.

aBOUT I

The real revenge.

Hearts beat faster in order to secure their presence.

If your heart starts racing in panic or sorrow, just know that it's because you neglected it one day.

Give the world time to heal.

It's been a rough four billion years.

The past generations were never as careless about the future generations as we are.

We all share the same loneliness.

If only we actually shared it.

I studied his creases—

Every piece of him—

Until me and death were one,

Until pieces of death were engraved inside me.

I wished it,

Inhaled it,

Crushed it,

Smoked it,

Took it in, in every way.

My body refuses to give in,

Refuses to admit that me and death are endless.

My body is yet to fight it in different ways,

Different toxins from my immune system.

Death regenerates as a thousand different viruses,

And my body won't give in until my last breath.

And so, until my last breath, my body will be fighting this part of me,

The part of me constructed by death.

As a child I thought

God was above us all,

And the devil lay beneath my feet.

I stand in the middle, free to choose either of them.

But how far is God compared to what lay under me?

Are we even half the people we pretend to be?

How come we call ourselves humans

When the closest thing we've come to humanity is by definition?

Even the stars lie; they shine, and then they die and reach us after a billion years.

Ever since life was born, death was its soulmate.

Everyday life gives death a present, yet he's always hungry for more.

She feeds everybody with delusions of happiness, success, and faith

Until they are filled with wisdom.

And then she hands them over to death, but death is always building walls between them.

However, life is so determined that death has more to offer,

Not knowing that death is waiting for her to be full of wisdom, so he can feed on her too.

When you start doubting your womanhood,

Remember that God created Eve because Adam needed her.

I wish the world flourishes and starts loving its own rhythm. Stops to listen how fulfilled it is with harmonies that it has taught us. Maybe then it's satisfaction will envelop us, and we will learn how to love ourselves again.

They taught me that I was not allowed to trust God with anything but my sins. Now only me and God carry them. How can I look God in the eye when I can't even look at myself?

The sun is always smiling, but the sea is always full of tears.

Now, every time I shower, I feel like I'm bathing myself with filtered sadness.

So the moon becomes much brighter to me.

It reflects its light to all the stars so they can shine too.

When they tell you to imagine the ocean, you think of me.

Waves thrusting through the shore, fighting to come first, but the current to you it ceases.

You're too busy focusing on the beach to bother looking at the ocean.

Allow him to feel what society didn't. Give him no borders for who he should be, and he will give you no borders for what he can do.

Toxic masculinity.

Don’t be enslaved to your own thoughts.

Let your origami heart unfold to those who desire it.

Pretend that the creases don't exist even after all this time.

Ignore that you know where you have been bent.

When they start folding over the original fold,

Stop them, and ask them to walk away.

And fold your origami heart into the exact shape it was.

Remember why it was folded in the first place,

And ignore the crease that they have created,

The one line that is out of its place.

Pretend it doesn't exist.

Let us fall in love with the simplicity of watching the waterfalls and the water touching itself while it moans.

Let's speak of the unspoken

while the ashes accumulate, resembling it, and

let us hope that the bottles fall over while the wind touches them in order to make them feel human;

let us hope we learn the meaning of laughter and laugh till the wilderness is not present anymore.

Just like us.

Let's bond over burnt ashes and cigarette buds.

The bigger picture.

Take a second, and listen to the earth's magnitude coming towards you.

Learn that it is alive as well.

It will teach you the meaning of life while playing symphonies of silence that gravitate in ways you never could.

Let us simply discuss the meanings behind our words. Let us build a fort where we surrender ourselves to the meaning of where we belong. Somewhere on this planet we have a home. Somewhere on this planet they will accept us. The longer you live, the more it feels like you weren't meant to taste peaches and creams. You were meant to eat ashes because this is not the place for you. Let's settle to a war. A war we will fight for us and the rest of us who may or may not survive somewhere we choose home, yet we choose to destroy. Happiness is merely what you make it. You learn to adapt it from others and to swallow your pride as if it didn't even belong to you in the first place. We are taught that if you don't choose to make a difference, you will never see change. But how come every time someone tries, they don't seem to possess the power? The power belongs to others who we choose to give it to in order to survive because some are evil. Some carry pain and neglect in their hearts. But what if those people just want the power and not to protect it. I'm exhausted of watching people sacrifice their lives at the cost of peace. I'm exhausted of watching children fight wars and crying while others film them. I wish I had the power to fight their fights for them, but there's only so much one can handle. Sit for a second and think. Is your home being stripped away from you while ashes pile up over dead bodies of the innocent? How are they to recognize where they belong when belonging is not even an option? How are we willing to give so much, yet it still seems as though they are so far from us? They lost, you didn't. You are privileged, but you lost the meaning of that word. You chose to lose it, but somewhere along the line, you need to open your eyes and see how important it is for you to live. Stop memorizing your own lines. They are there, fighting wars that were meant for all of us. They are there dying because we lost what is ours.

I wish we knew how valuable these moments were when we had them.

The sense of belonging we once had is now fading.

Belonging now means new people.

We are so busy discovering ourselves, we often forget others are too.

Belonging now has become a part of us, a constant hunger for satisfaction.

Belonging now makes us feel incomplete. We grew so distant from the rest of the world, even though we are all a part of each other.

Belonging now makes us selfish; we think that giving is a part of taking back.

Belonging now means searching for a place to sit, while everyone around us is standing.

Belonging is us.

About Sarcasm

What doesn't kill you kills you from the inside.

Emotions are underrated.

You don't need his hoodies; you can get your own from the men's section.

There isn't enough depression in this world to fit the population.

Thank you for ruining so many perfectly average songs for me.

Drowning in memes I'd like to share with just you.

Ladies, if you know what you could do to yourself, you'd stop looking for it in other people.

I would like to enlighten a part of the population.

According to *Oxford Dictionaries* (2019), the definition of no is, "Not any.

'there is no excuse'."

Oh, it doesn't say, "Convince me"? Or, "Try harder"?

How mesmerizing.

A poem.

F**k you.

The end.

I'm a whore.

Sue me.

I want to get lost in the land of unfound socks and hair ties.

Honey, crying is for men.

But we were supposed go on plane rides together.

She was addicted to her phone because you were on it.

Where’s the fun in easy, precious?

Finally,

We all think of how fire burns but forget that water can burn fire.

We are creatures of habit.

When you walked away,

He became my creature of habit.

The first time I had an anxiety attack,

I realized that you can only think so much about breathing until you forget how to do it.

I often wonder why people are afraid of the dark.

Darkness is like a canvas for imagination.

You can't see what's happening, but you can paint it and make it come to life.

It's 3 a.m. where you belong.

I knew it wasn't me anymore.

It's 3 a.m. where I belong, where I learned the language of my own demons.

I let them admire me while they whisper my flaws.

They like my tears.

They taught me to like my tears, and so I admired them, secretly.

Somehow sins seem to dissolve when you're the only one who knows about them.

If nostalgia was a person Nostalgia,

she would interlace herself onto you and bat her eyelashes and have the softest voice; and she would murmur in your ear how much she loved you while holding a knife to your gut.

If nostalgia was a person, she would view your sins for the whole world to see, just so she could be the only one there for you.

If nostalgia was a person, she would creep under your sheets and memorize your body till she could finally touch all your weaknesses; and you let her do it, even though it's painful every time, and you start growing bruises night after night.

If nostalgia was a person, you wouldn't be able to resist her smile.

She wears it so nicely.

Don't blame yourself after nostalgia touches you. But you can't blame her either; nostalgia will only be present if you don't ask her to go. And if you can't resist her, remind yourself of all these people nostalgia has manipulated. Welcome her with open arms; she will have to leave eventually.

Who needs you?

The road slowly started to dip into waves behind us while we drove straight to our own misery. I looked at your gaze—focused, unphased. The moment you realized I was looking at you, your demeanour slowly started to rise to the occasion, realizing it's just us. For once, it was only us we had to worry about. The rest of the world was recycled into bits of us that we could not command. I held your hand, although your hand mimicked his grip. His was much stronger, deeper. Yours was weak; he didn't need me. You, you just let me know how aware you were of my existence. How soft you chose to become because you needed and not wanted me. You were asking me to pick you up, but I know your sins. You tried to bury them, but I was a part of them.

I stared directly at the broken parts of the road, and I knew they were telling a story. They were asking to be repaired; you were asking to be repaired. He didn't know he needed repairing; he didn't want to admit to all he was carrying. Eventually he was right. He walked away; I had unfolded so much to someone who wasn't ready. You, you were soft. You tried to tell me you could handle it. But after all that he had done, I chose to bury them and never to dig again. "He did that to me," I said. But he wasn't the one who compromised his happiness. He wasn't the one who chose to unravel himself to someone he knew was temporary. The road told a story. It carried its own pride, and despite being damaged, it let those who pleased swift over it with the heavy weight of their machinery. Knowing that it might have nudged them a little bit, being aware that it was not completing its duties like the others. But the road spoke and said, “At least I am here while others may have collapsed.”

I let her be in love with me because she earned it.

I let her be in love with me because how can you not love someone whose only purpose in life is to love you?

So he let me be in love with him.

Not realizing that my love and even his will destroy us.

He let me be in love with him; he embraced it like he only learned to admire, to adapt, to want.

They let us be in love with each other.

Not realizing that we loved each other.

They watched from a distance.

What if when you touch love, you create a nuclear explosion? One that is so beautiful you forget the damage it makes.

I was so busy dying that living was part of it.

I ignore the dotted lines on the page, and I simply begin to write. I let the words infiltrate each other, creating patterns that embody my pain.

From the heart I said,

"We are waterfalls."

Some vows are unspoken ones. If they are broken, you do not have the right to say anything. How come it still hurts just as much? Some vows are unspoken ones; that does not mean they have the right to be broken.

How can you love someone so loudly and still give up on them? I guess you were numb from the screaming.

I'm lying on a table of sins that seems to envelop me.

If every moment we had was suffused with silence, maybe then words would be rare and beautiful.

Somehow, I should always be the closest yet the furthest thing to you.

You want to know how I am, but you never want to ask me.

So you start plucking the petals in the rosebud that is my life,

Not realizing that it is not yet spring, and you're forcing my flower to bloom,

Trying to infiltrate the natural process of its growth.

You are a murderer.

Allow me to forget that we shared the same breath of air while floating between the headlights of an unknown city.

You are a murderer.

An embodiment of the axeman, his rebirth,

Always trying to be one step ahead of me just in case I decide to race again.

But my knees are already displacing, and I ran out of breath.

I just want to grow my rose again without you snatching its roots and tasting it with the glide of your fingers, trying to memorize its veins and patterns so you can cut off where it feeds. Just like a murderer.

You are appreciated by others while they watch you be the wittiest, but they will despise you when you pluck their flower.

Leave me grow, without you.

Our hands don't fit so perfectly anymore. Instead, you place your palm on the outline of my cheek. And I push my jaw so it rests perfectly between your fingers, reminding myself that my vertebrate can support itself.

Without the trace of your long, monster-like fingertips.

Shallow.

The lights tend to reflect on the ocean and flutter with its current, no matter what direction you put them in.

Be the ocean.

I want to paint a painting with only black paint. As dark as the sky during the day. And the brightest it could ever be during the night.

Don't call me beautiful.

They told me I was beautiful.

I felt them skin me alive,

Watched the knives tear through the layers of my skin.

And so I was their act of butchery.

I watched parts of me become theirs, and they called me names,

Kept calling me, "That girl."

Claimed it was the truth.

And so I laughed.

I laughed at their vulnerability and their ignorance.

I laughed because I knew better.

I laughed because I knew that the only truth in life is death.

They made me forget my name

Until that girl was my identity.

They said,

"I wish I had a girl like you, with a religious and a fun side.

A girl who doesn't take everything too seriously.

And so jealousy was portrayed as an act of butchery.

Suffuse your burnt book with your own filth.

Do not make me part of your gaping hands and fingers.

They told me I was beautiful.

Didn't teach me how to peruse beauty

Or portray it.

They didn't tell me, and so I am telling you,

Don't mould yourself into beauty

Or let beauty mould into you.

It's already there.

Every single part of you is beautiful.

So when someone tries to define you,

Tell them that you possess your own story.

Call them stupid, call them stupid for believing tales that were passed through way too many tongues to be believed.

The next time someone tells you, you are beautiful,

Tell them to call you smart or ambitious or intuitive.

ABOUT THE AUTHOR

Sarah AA is a newly developing author who always aims to say everything that everyone else is afraid to say. She also likes to have a hint of sarcasm in most of her work for those who know how to read between the lines.